LEADERSHIP:

POWER, PROCESS AND MANAGEMENT

GETTING YOURSELF FIT FOR THE NEXT TASK

By:

John S. Coughlin

TABLE OF CONTENT

INTRODUCTION

Leadership is crucial not only because it determines the management style, but also because achieving corporate objectives depends on the managers' ability to gain the commitment of the subordinates.

Leadership is a managerial function. For example, the directing (i.e. leading) function of an editor requires him to conduct himself a way that reporters and other editorial staff's job performance and moral will remain high. Therefore, managers must understand the nature of leadership for effectiveness.

CHAPTER ONE

LEADERSHIP

Many definitions of leadership have been given by management scholars some of which are that:

- It is the process of influencing others to work willingly, to achieve organisational goal, rather than out of far.
- It is a dynamic process in a group whereby one individual influences others to contribute to the achievement of group tasks.
- Leardeship is both a process and a property. The process is the use of non-coercive influence to direct and coordinate the activities of a group for

the accomplishment of its objectives. As property, leadership is the set of qualities or characteristics attributed to those who are perceived to successfully employ such influence.

- It is the influential increment over and above mechanical compliance with the routine directives of the organisation.

The definitions above show that leadership is a dynamic process and that influence emanates from the leader who direct subordinates towards goal achievement. However, this traditional belief that influence flows from the leader has changed since it was discovered that in complex organisation, influence flows not only from the top down but also from the bottom up. For example, the news editor may give news stories written by reporters believed to be incompetent close scrutiny, but gave less supervision to that of those adjusted experienced and competent. This shows how reporters' performance can influence a leader.

Again, the news editor, having the authority to re-deploy or sack a reporter considered intemperate and rude, may accommodate such a reporter's behaviour by giving him assignments that do not involve much interpersonal relationship with news sources. He can make him spend more time on the desk than on the field. These examples show the complexity of interaction between leaders and subordinate in a media organisation or any other organisation and how subordinate' attitude may influence the leadership behaviour of the editors.

Another aspect of leadership process that must be understood is that a manager holding a formal position may not necessarily be a leader. For example, though the news editor is the manager in the newsroom of a newspaper organisation because of his formal authority, a leader on the other hand may be an individual other than the news editor who influences others to get the job done. It is the ability of the news editor to inspire his reporters to do their jobs willingly that marks him out as a leader. It is a case that the informal leader of a department is one who influences colleagues' behaviours; while the formal leader is the formal head of the department. While it is possible for the informal leader to be the formal leader, the assumption of informal leadership is not automatic for the formal leader.

It must be pointed out that a leader in any department enjoys his roles and position because of the recognition given to him by the subordinates and the top management. His authority may be technically withdrawn if this group refuses to recognise him. It is in view of this that the manager and others must rely on their personality and expert power other than position power alone this reality leads us to the concept of power and its relationship with the leadership process.

CHAPTER TWO

POWER

Power is an individual's ability to influence other people and events. Leaders obtain it through their personalities, positions and the circumstances they find themselves. For example, the manager derives their authority over subordinates from various power base, some of which are discussed below:

a) **Coercive power-** This kind of power is rooted in fear and threats of punishment. It is often used by leaders to get job done. In an organisation, staffs work themselves to the bones in order not to miss bonus. They do this to avoid being queried or sacked. Some of them get the job done to prevent being shouted at by the manager. Presenters and producers in the electronic media do the same in submission to coercive power of their bosses.

b) **Legitimate power:** This is position power gained by the formal authority conferred on an individual by the top management or any higher authority on the hierarchy. The manager or principal allocates assignments to subordinate with instructions on how they should be carried out and expects his orders to be obeyed within stipulated time. He has legitimate power to do so.

c) **Referent power:** This is derived from the personal qualities of charisma of the leader. The admiration engendered by these qualities induces their limitation by subordinate. Staffs often admire some manager for their enterprising nature, firmness, punctuality, good dressing habit, etc. and consciously or unconsciously take after them. This form of power enables the manager to gain easy compliance to his wish because he is admired and liked.

d) **Expert Power:** This is power derived from the leader's possession of relevant expertise, skill and knowledge of the job. Producers, presenters and reporters respect and obey leaders which have good knowledge of the job. In addition, an individual in an editorial department of a newspaper organisation or programmed section of a television station may be influential because of his expertise, even when he lacks the seniority to wield formal authority.

e) **Reward Power:** This power confers on an individual the authority to give rewards, like promotion, recognition and increased pay to subordinates who comply with his orders. This power base is often cause by sycophancy, and false loyalty to staffs and managers.

f) **Connection Power:** This is power derived from informal links with eminent individuals who have controlling shares in an organisation. The closeness of the manager to the proprietor, or a powerful member of the board of directors, or even the managing director, can boost his power base. In used excessively, connection power will induce fear and, therefore, pretended loyalty, which may be counter-productive.

g) **Political Power**: This form of power is derived from the support given by group members. For example, some leaders in trade unions or politics are elected to positions of power. A reporter, or a programme production staff, may be feared or recognised by the management because he is the chairman of the Journalists' Union. The position enables him to rally workers in support or against management policies as the situation demands.

h) **Information Power**: The liaison role between the top management and subordinate performed by the leader enables him to gather information about management plans and thinking on certain issues. Therefore, he may engage in strategic release or withdrawal of information to manipulate subordinate. For example, the manager and others may play politics with information in their possession in order to delay speed up decision-making by subordinate on certain matters.

CHAPTER THREE

TYPES OF LEADERSHIP

Below are the various types of leadership with reflections of some of the power discussed above:

a) **The Charismatic Leader**- The influence wielded by this type of leader emanates mainly from his personal qualities. The only problem is that, not everybody possesses exceptional attributes that can transform others into willing followers. Moreover, these attributes cannot be acquired by formal teaching. Jesus Christ, Napoleon, Winston Churchill are examples of charismatic leaders. A charismatic manager is bound to have great influence on others and subordinates.

b) **The Situation Leader-** This is a temporary type of leadership whose effectiveness depends on his being in the right place at the right time. The transient nature of this kind of leadership makes it inappropriate for an individual concern, since what is needed is a leader who can play leadership role in different situations foe an extended period.

c) **The Traditional Leader-** This is an ascribed status, since leadership is a function of birth. For example, kingship or queenship is a position conferred by birth into a royal family which makes it impossible for many to aspire to it.

d) **The Appointed Leader-** The position occupied confers leadership role on this individual. In other words, the legitimate power wielded by this type of leader is function of his formal authority within the hierarchy,

e) The Functional Leader- For this type of leader, what he does determines his leadership position, rather than what he is. For example, effective leadership depends on what he does to meet task, group and individual needs. He may task needs by allocation responsibilities and settings performance standards or meet group needs by acting as a representative. At individual level, he may choose to counsel or motivate individuals.

CHAPTER FOUR
LEADERSHIP STYLES AND THEIR IMPLICATIONS

Leadership style can be defined as the behaviour exhibited by a leader during supervision of subordinates. The style is a function of his assumption about his subordinates and his behaviour when interacting with them.

While a leader can exercise his authority in many ways, it must be noted that style determines the degree of motivation, efficiency and effectiveness of subordinates. Though, there are as many leadership styles as there are leaders, the four major styles are:

a) **Dictatorial Style-** This style involves the use of force and threats by the manager to make subordinates carry out official assignments. There is immense use of coercion in task execution.

b) **The Autocratic Styles-** Here decision-making is centralised in the leader's hands, while subordinates participation is discouraged. It is a 'tell style' characterized by one-way communication. The leader tells subordinates what to do but not why they must do it. This style kills subordinate's' initiatives and lowers moral and commitment to work.

In a media organisation, the editor and others managers adopting te style make decision and announce them. They sell decision to subordinates and ask for comment, which they may not use. In many organisations the bencvolent variant of this leadership is often adopted with the editor formulating policies and discarding advice from subordinates because he believes the decision is for the good of the organisation. However, real autocratic style prevails in any organisation owned by individual who, in most cases, expects things done his own way. The manager's reasons for adopting autocratic style may be due to the feeling that subordinates are incompetent and lazy. One benefit of this style is that assignments are executed to deadlines, since consultation with subordinates will not constitute an impediment.

c) **The Democratic (Participative) style-** Unlike the autocratic style decision-making is decentralised. It is also called 'join style'. The leader delegate's responsibility to subordinates according to competence ad interest, its success depends on tier willingness to participate. Managers adopting this style suggest sketched ideas and ask for contributions, or present a problem and ask for ideas to enable them adjust their own position on it.

The advantages of this style are: it boosts the feeling of self-worth and satisfaction in employees; it makes the, feel self-actualised through participation in decision-making; the input made by employees may improve the quality of decision-making, and lastly, change implementation will be easier because of subordinates' input.

d) **The Laissez – faire style of the 'abdicratic' style-** This style also called the 'free rein style' or that of 'anything goes' is that whereby a leader, rather than assume leadership roles, abdicates the position by giving it to someone else. Technically, it is said not to be a leadership style, but more of an absence of one, since it portrays a scenario whereby subordinates are given little or no direction, but allowed to establish their own objectives and make all decision.

A leader may adopt the 'abdicratic style' due to lack of self-confidence, fear of non-performance and personal evaluation of the costs of leading which may outweigh the advantages.

Managers may adopt this style if they believe allowing their subordinate's greater use of initiatives will enhance job performance. Besides, it may be a better option where subordinates are highly motivated, experienced and competent. In that case, the manager will present a problem and ask them to solve it as they wish within specified limits.

CHAPTER FIVE

QUALITIES OF A GOOD LEADER

A good leader must have the following characteristics, which constitute the 'eleven secret of leadership' given by Napoleon Hill, in his work. **Think and Grow Rich.**

a) **Unwavering courage** – This is essential because no intelligent follower wants to be dominated by a leader who lacks self-confidence and courage,

b) **Self-control** – An individual unable to control himself cannot control others. Possession of self-control by the manager is a good example for his subordinates.

c) **A keen sense of justice-** No leader can retain the respect of his subordinates without a sense of fairness and justices.

d) **Decisiveness-** The person who wavers in his decisions shows that he is not sure of himself and, therefore, cannot lead others.

e) **Habit of doing more than paid for** – The willingness to do more than even tie followers is a penalty of leadership. The manager must be ready to work harder or show greater commitment to work than subordinates.

f) **Pleasant Personality** – Followers will respect a leader who has a pleasant personality. Managers or individuals must be amiable and possess good human relations.

g) **Sympathy and understanding** – Must understand the problems of his subordinates and sympathise as appropriate.

h) **Mastery of details** – Successfully leadership calls for mastery of details about one's position.

i) **Willingness to assume full responsibility** – A good leader must be prepared to assume responsibility for the mistakes and shortcomings of his followers.

j) **Co-operation** – He must be able to apply the principle of co[operative effort and induce same in his subordinates.

In addition, to the qualities given above, **Ralph Stogdhill** in his classic work published in 1948, reviewed 124 empirical studies of leader attribute covering twenty-seven recurring characteristics. In these studies, he discovered some consistency. Some of the characteristics he claimed successful leaders generally exhibited are:

a) **Height** - Leaders tended to be taller than the average height of the followers.
b) **Intelligence** - Leaders tended to be rated higher on intelligent quotient (IQ) tests, covering verbal fluency, overall knowledge, originality and insight.
c) **Initiative** – Leaders tended to show high level of energy, ambition and persistence.

However, no clear relationship was found between a leader's success and characteristics like emotional stability or extroversion.

Other things discovered by Stogdhill, which subsequently led to more comprehensive research are that in many instances, the profile of a successful leader varied with the situation. This means that different groups and different group activities required different types of leaders. This discovery eventually led in the early 1950s, to the study of how leaders interacted with group under various conditions and how they succeeded or failed.

CHAPTER SIX
LEADERSHIP THEORIES

Two sets of theories will be discussed here. The first set is Universalist theories, which argues that a single style of leadership is suitable for all situations. The other one is contingency theories anchored on basic assumption that different situations require different leadership styled for effectiveness. The theories also recognise the impact of environment and individual differences factors on leadership behaviour.

Universalist Theories

a) The Great Man Approach

The earliest and simplest view of leadership was that leaders are born and that qualities like great vision, competence and good personality which marked out historical figures like Jesus Christ, Winston Churchill, Alexander the Great, Joan of Arc, were inherited. The theory adds that the frequency with which great personalities are found in certain families suggests genetic origin of leadership. Such personalities, it was sais, are destined for positions of influence.

This approach has been criticized for many reasons, one of the criticisms is that its acceptance may lead to a legitimation of favouritism in staff promotion as relations of past successful leaders move into an organisation. Besides, of the view that 'leaders are born, not made' is accepted, then organizations must recruit only born leaders into their workforce whereas this is impossible and accepting it will make management training programme irrelevant since recruited staff will be born leaders who may not need further training.

b) The Trait Approach

This approach is similar in a way to be 'great man' approach. For example, it relies on the assumption that the personality traits of a leader are essential for leadership success. But the dissimilarity is that it does not emphasize that leaders are born with these personality traits but that certain traits, whether innate or acquired are essential for successful leadership.

The problem with this approach is that is it often difficult to measure certain traits.

For examplc, 'intelligence' which is a quality of a successful leader is difficult to measure. Also, while physical attributes like 'height', 'appearance' are observable, psychological ones like 'perseverance' 'initiative' 'intelligence' are not. Since the psychological attributes are not observable, their presence can only be inferred from behaviour, which is vulnerable to questionable conclusions. Moreover, traits possessed by successful leaders are often value-judged as positive (e.g. decisive, intelligence, strong, e.t.c.) whereas most leaders often exhibit negative qualities, which are not directly listed.

c) The Managerial Grid

The failure of the traits approach to differentiate successfully traits that could distinguish successful leaders form non-successful ones, led to a shift of emphasis from traits to leader behaviours.

Two leader behaviour styles emphasized by Blake and Mouton (1978) are:

a) Concern for the people(i.e. people – centered)
b) Concern for production (i.e. production - centered)

The five managerial grids identified by them bear some similarities with some of the leadership styles earlier discussed. They are:

1, 1 Style: This is impoverished style of management. It corresponds with the laissez – faire leadership style where the leader puts in minimum effort to get the work done. Here, the manager cares little for both the employee and production. A manager employing the style provides little leadership or direction for subordinates. He allows subordinates greater discretion.

1, 9 Style: Called the country-club management style, it shows how concern for production, but a high one for employees' or people's needs. The manager adopting this style exhibits good human relations at work. He excludes friendliness in his bid to seek social acceptance.

9, 1 Style: Referred to as authority – obedience style, the manager manifests authoritarian leadership because of his high concern for production and low concern of employees. Managers regarded ad 'slave-drivers' at work fit into this category. They are mostly concerned with meeting production target and in the process overstretch their subordinate. They have morbid fear of failure and so use their authority to ensure deadlines are met.

5, 5 **Style:** Called the organisation- men management. It is middle – of – the – road style involving a delicate balance between concern for production and employee satisfaction. The manager and other want production target to be met without losing face among their colleagues.

9, 9 Style: This is a team management or democratic leadership style. Here the manager shows a high concern for both people and production in media organisation; the editor and heads of unit adopting it carry others along in their efforts to meet production targets.

Blake and Mouton identified the 9, 9 style as the most desirable because of the high concern for both people and production. However, this view provides the basic for criticism as critics says that the belief that there is one leadership styles inherently superior to others is contrary to the contingency idea of leadership.

Summary of the five Managerial Grids

Style Label	Production	People
1, 1	Low	Low
9, 1	High	Low
1, 9	Low	High
5, 5	Moderate	Moderate
9, 9	High	High

CHAPTER SEVEN

CONTINGENY THEORIES

Unlike the Universalist theories, the contingency theories take into consideration the complexities of leadership behaviours. For example, they assume that leadership theories must consider environmental and individual differences factors. Besides, they emphasize that a leader's ability to lead, or influence his subordinates at work, depends on his adaptation of styles to various situations.

a) The Situational leadership theory

The theory developed by Hersey and Blanchard identifies two sets of behaviours. They are 'relationship behaviour' and 'task behaviour'.

Relationship behaviour refers to the extent to which a leader engages in two-way communication with subordinates. It includes the extent to which subordinates are provided with emotional supports, encourage and other facilitating behaviour.

Task behaviour means that extent to which subordinates are giving direction and guidance such as telling them what to do, how to do it, and when to do it.

The two behaviours occur in various degrees. For example the manager can exhibit more task behaviour than relationship behaviour and vice versa. Henry and Blanchard, however derived four basic leadership styles from the combination of task and relationship behaviours. They are

High task, low relationship	=	***Telling style***
High task, high relationship	=	***Selling style***
Low task, high relationship	=	***Participating style***

Lot task, low relationship = *Delegating style*

The four styles, they say, can only be effective in varied situations and that their effectiveness depends on the maturity level of the subordinates, maturity level in this case means the ability and willingness of the people to assume responsibility for their own behaviour. A subordinate ,ay perform well on a specific task and thus needs less supervision, in that areas; but his performance may be poor in another area, needing supervision, until he matures.

b) The Leadership contingency Model

One of the most popular contemporary theories is the contingency theory advanced by Fred Fiedler (1976). It says that group performance of effectiveness is a function of interaction between leadership style and the favourableness of the situation (i.e. the environment). The three environmental variables he identifies as interacting with leadership styles to determine leadership effectiveness are:

a) **Leader- member relations** – This refers to the degree of confidence and respect subordinates have in their leader. One may find out whether the leader is accepted by and subordinates or relates well with them. In media organisations, editors and other managers who relates well with their subordinates find them easy to influence and subordinates have high regards for them.

b) **Task structure** – it refers to the degree to which task goals and roles assignment are clearly stated. The relevant questions to be asked by the manager are: Does every subordinate know what to do? Is there any ambiguity in their job? What goals are there to be attained? How can they be attained?

c) **Position power** – It refers to the formal authority held by the leader. The more rewards and punishment leaders can use the more influence they will have. The managing director of an organisation has more access to rewards and punishment than his subordinate. However, the power of the manager as the head of the department to hire and fire is greater than that of his subordinate.

(c) The Path – Goal Model

This model formulated by Robert House, assumes that leaders' behaviour can influence task performance by showing subordinates how performance can lead to the achievement of cooperate goals. The model draws on the expectancy theory of motivation. For example, it stresses the point that satisfactory leadership behaviour increase goal attainment by subordinates and even clarified that paths to those goals (i.e. expectancy).

To promote subordinates satisfaction in task accomplishment, a leader may withhold directive behaviour or guidance, if workers believe that they are capable of executing the assignment using their own initiatives. This behaviour will boost their satisfaction, while directives behaviour on the other hand will cause dissatisfaction because it is unnecessary.

Another aspect of the model is that relating to clarification of task characteristics and expectations in order to reduce ambiguity. When task performance is well defined for jobs, goal attainment becomes clearer, since there will be no uncertainty. In addition, when routine jobs are infused with task variety, work becomes more satisfying and frustrations reduce.

CHAPTER EIGHT

IMPROVING LEADERSHIP EFFECTIVENESS

While leadership is not the only solution to performance problems in organisations, top managers must, nevertheless, put in place an arrangement that can facilitate leadership effectiveness. Some of the strategies that can be adopted are:

a) **Rewarding Leader Behaviour**. Leadership effectiveness can be improved when good reward systems are designed to compensate managers for their ability to move their subordinate successfully towards goal-directed activities. Through this, managers will realize the importance of leadership in task accomplishment and always seek for improvement. For example, generous pay and promotion can be liked to good leader behaviour.

b) **Rewarding subordinate behaviour** – Reward system can also be structured to stimulate subordinate behaviour. For example, managers can be empowered to reward subordinate. This may increase future compliance with managerial directive since this can enhance their own personal goal attainment.

c) **Careful managerial selection and practice** - This involves matching people with leadership roles. A tsk-oriented leader can be made to supervise a work-group characterized by high-task structuring, centralised power and distant leader-member relations. Likewise, a relationship-oriented leader is more useful when the task structuring is less concrete and requires leader-member relations.

d) **Organisational Engineering** – This involves engineering (or re-designing) the job to fit the manager. In some cases, leadership effectives can be achieved when the manager, or any other manager's job is modified, or the reporting procedures, line of authority is structured to facilitate task execution. This approach may be necessary when the services of such manager is valued, but lacks the interpersonal; skills of leadership. In that case, the job can be engineered around him for successful performance. This view is supported by

Fielder who says that, instead of attempting to induce behavioural changes in the leader, it is better to adapt the situation to his style.

e) **Leadership Training** - Managers can be assisted to develop their leadership potentials to the fullest through training schemes, which may include problem solving and decision making training, general management skills training, human relations training and other specialized training programmes, which can facilitate effective newsroom management and goal-achievement behaviour.

CONCLUSION

It is needful to learn and understand the qualities and capacity of leaders in present business scenario. Knowledge of strength and weaknesses and the areas where the complimentary skills and strength can be brought to develop in a better way may be considered. The essential qualities of leaders may be created and developed by way of personal development,

A learning process may be developed to know about the multiple socio-culture environment and to know about the wide range of spectrum of life styles in the society. The emotional competencies also generates and sustains trust, empathy, belongingness and morale value in leadership development,

Within the leadership development process, there is a need to avoid and discourage the autocratic behaviour, monopolistic attitude, social evils, resistance to change, unethical norms in organisation and different critical approaches in organizations. The leadership styles may develop the humanitarian ground which is duly based on employee oriented aspects in the organisation.

www.ingramcontent.com/pod-product-compliance
Lightning Source LLC
LaVergne TN
LVHW020524160826
845677LV00015B/3891

* 9 7 9 8 8 4 8 6 2 4 2 0 5 *